EDGE BOOKS™

Fantastically FUNNY TRICKS

by Norm Barnhart

CAPSTONE PRESS
a capstone imprint

Edge Books are published by Capstone Press,
1710 Roe Crest Drive, North Mankato, Minnesota 56003
www.capstonepub.com

Copyright © 2014 by Capstone Press, a Capstone imprint. All rights reserved.
No part of this publication may be reproduced in whole or in part, or stored in a
retrieval system, or transmitted in any form or by any means, electronic, mechanical,
photocopying, recording, or otherwise, without written permission of the publisher.

Library of Congress Cataloging-in-Publication Data
Barnhart, Norm.
Fantastically funny tricks / by Norm Barnhart.
pages cm.—(Edge books. Magic manuals)
Includes bibliographical references.
Summary: "Step-by-step instructions and photos show how to do a variety of fun and
entertaining comedy tricks"—Provided by publisher.
ISBN 978-1-4765-0136-9 (library binding)
ISBN 978-1-4765-3392-6 (ebook PDF)
1. Tricks—Juvenile literature. I. Title.
GV1548.B363 2014
793.8—dc23   2013004919

Editorial Credits
Aaron Sautter, editor; Tracy Davies McCabe, designer; Svetlana Zhurkin,
media researcher; Jennifer Walker, production specialist; Sarah Schuette,
photo stylist; Marcy Morin, photo scheduler

Photo Credits
All interior photos by Capstone Studio/Karon Dubke.
Cover and background images by Shutterstock/Anna Subbotina, Chin Kit Sen,
Creatista, Dimec, Sergey Furtaev, Valentin Agapov, and Veerachai Viteeman.

Printed in the United States of America in Stevens Point, Wisconsin.
032013   007227WZF13

TABLE OF CONTENTS

Make Them Laugh! 4

Have A Chip! 6

Funny Flower 8

Excellent Flying Eggs 11

Party in a Box 14

Washday Wonder 18

Ping-Pong Surprise! 20

Phooey Shoey 23

Key of Mystery 26

The Dancing Hanky 28

Read More 32

Internet Sites 32

MAKE THEM LAUGH!

Comedy and magic go together like peanut butter and jelly. Audiences love watching magicians who make them laugh. Whether you're performing simple card tricks or incredible illusions, unexpected surprises can add laughter and fun to your show.

Every person has his or her own comic style. Think about things that make you laugh. You will likely be good at that kind of comedy. You might like to tell jokes or say witty comments to get a laugh. Or maybe you're better at being silly than witty.

Whatever your style, practice the following tips to get the audience laughing:

▸ **Tell a Story:** Share a funny story using silly or mysterious voices to spark people's imaginations.

▸ **Use Funny Faces:** Your face is your most useful tool. Funny facial expressions grab people's attention and help you communicate with the audience.

▸ **Use Physical Comedy:** People often get a good laugh at the physical reactions of others. Try ducking or jumping back in surprise as if a trick hasn't turned out the way you expected.

Magic Secret: The Magician's Case

Magicians often use a special magic box or case in their shows. Magic cases can be very useful They provide a place to keep props and other items. Magicians often use cases to hide objects from an audience. Many of the tricks in this book use a magic case. You can make your own case out of a cardboard box or an old suitcase. Make it look fancy or old and beat up. Add some sparkly cloth to make it look sharp and magical. Or cover it with stickers to look like you've been on a world tour.

TIP: Put some cardboard dividers in the case to keep your props organized. This will help your tricks go smoothly during your show.

Have A CHiP!

This trick will give your friends a good scare. When they reach into your bag of chips, a hand pops out of the bag to grab them!

What You Need:
- a chip bag
- a few chips
- scissors

PREPARATION:

1. Empty the chips out of the bag. Then cut a hole in the back of the bag large enough to fit your hand through.

2. Place a few chips inside the bag.

TIP: After you do this trick for one friend, you can try it on a new person. The first friend can take a chip from the bag and eat it normally. Then you can offer the bag to the new person. Everyone will enjoy the person's shock and surprise when you grab his or her hand!

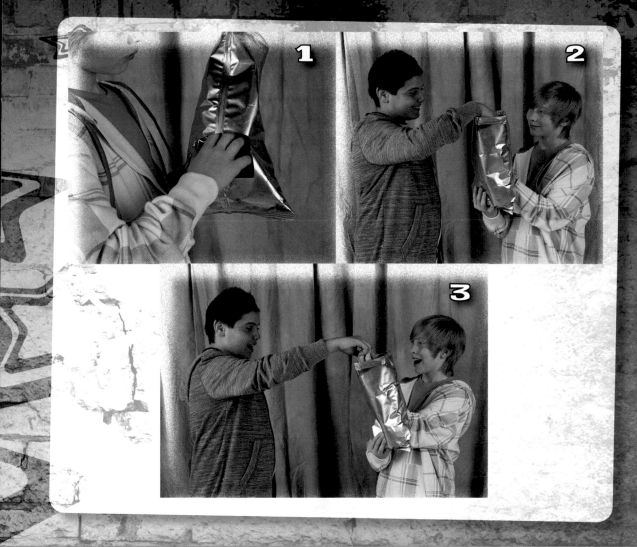

PERFORMANCE:

1. Take the chip bag out of your magic case. As you do this, slide your hand into the hole at the back of the bag. Show the bag to your friends and say, "This is a brand new snack. The bag lets only the owner eat the chips inside."

2. Ask someone to try to take a chip out of the bag. Say, "Feel free to have some chips—if you can. The bag will keep you from getting any."

3. When the volunteer reaches for the bag, grab his or her hand with your hidden hand. The person won't expect it and will get a good scare. The audience will get a good laugh as the volunteer jumps back in surprise!

Funny Flower

Is that a flower in your hat? Your friends will try to help you make a flower magically grow in a pot. But they'll get a big laugh when they see the flower grows in your hat instead!

What You Need:
- a small flowerpot
- a hat
- a silk flower
- magic wand

PREPARATION:

1. Place the flower inside the hat. Keep the hat and flowerpot inside your magic case.

PERFORMANCE:

1. Take out the hat and flowerpot. Hide the flower by covering it with your fingers against the side of the hat as shown (1a). Tip the hat to show the audience it is empty (1b). Then place the hat on your head so the flower will be in place at the end of the trick.

TIP: When people toss invisible soil and water at you, pretend that you are getting hit with it. Your reactions can bring a lot of laughter.

2. Reach into your pocket and pretend to take out some magic invisible flower seeds. Hold out your empty hand to the audience and say, "With a little magic, these invisible flower seeds grow really fast. Let's grow one in the pot." Pretend to place some of the invisible seeds into the pot.

3. Take out your magic wand. Then wave it at the flowerpot and say some magic words like, "Flora, fauna, foo!" Look at the pot as if you expect the flower to grow. Then act disappointed when nothing happens.

4. Say, "Oh, wait. We need some magic soil." Hold up the pot and ask the audience to toss invisible soil into it. Put down the pot, wave the magic wand, and say the magic words again. Once again, nothing happens.

5. Say, "Oh, I forgot. The seeds need water too." Pretend to sprinkle invisible water in the pot. Repeat the magic words again. But still nothing happens.

6. Say, "I know—we need sunshine!" Ask the audience to wave their fingers and send magic sunshine toward the flowerpot. Repeat the magic words again. Once again, look confused or disappointed when nothing happens. Then tap the magic wand on your head as if you are thinking.

7. Pretend that something is happening inside your hat. Lift the hat up to show the flower sitting on top of your head. Act surprised and say, "Hey, you made the seeds grow in my hat!"

EXCELLENT FLYING EGGS

Eggs are great for breakfast. But if you aren't careful, they can make a big mess. This trick will have people jumping and laughing when fake eggs fly into the crowd.

What You Need:
- medium-sized marshmallows
- an egg carton
- one white plastic egg
- a hat
- a magic wand
- a long table

PREPARATION:

1. Fill the egg carton with the marshmallows and one plastic egg.

TIP: Pretend the egg carton is filled with real eggs. Handle the carton carefully. Act like you don't want to drop it and break the eggs inside. Acting this way helps the audience believe you are using real eggs for this trick.

PERFORMANCE:

1. Take out the egg carton and place it on one end of the table. Take out the plastic egg and show it to the audience. Say, "Who'd like to see this egg magically travel through the air?"

2. Place the hat on the other end of the table. Then place the egg in the hat. Wave the magic wand over the hat first, and then the egg carton. Look into the egg carton, but don't let the crowd see inside. Say, "Yep, the egg is in there."

3. Repeat Step 2 and pretend to send the egg back to the hat. Take the egg out of the hat and show it with a "Ta-da!" motion. The audience won't be impressed. Say, "Did you miss it? Let's try it again." Repeat the process again to send the egg to the carton.

4. Say, "Now we'll send the egg back to the hat!" The audience won't like this because they didn't get to see the egg in the carton. They'll probably say, "We don't believe the egg moved. Show us the egg in the carton."

5. Act as if you forgot to show the audience the egg. Say, "Oh yes, of course. I promise the egg is in the carton. Let me show you." Pick up the carton and pretend that the lid is stuck. Pretend to fumble with the carton for a bit to get it open.

6. Finally, flip the lid open and toss the carton in the air to make the marshmallows fly into the crowd. People will think the marshmallows are real eggs and duck out of the way. But they'll get a big laugh when they see the eggs are just marshmallows. Tell the audience, "Oh, so that's where I put those!"

TRICK FOUR
Party in a Box

You can be the life of the party! This trick is great to use at the beginning of your show to get the audience in the right mood.

What You Need:
- a large shoebox
- 1 foot (0.3 meter) of strong string
- strong clear tape
- a strong metal binder clip
- party toys like kazoos, balloons, and noise makers
- a large, colorful handkerchief
- a magic wand
- colorful confetti
- a table and a colorful tablecloth

PREPARATION:

1. Decorate the shoebox with bright colors. Write "Party in a Box" on the top.

2. Tightly tie one end of the string to the strong clip. Tape the other end inside the back of the box.

3. Place the party toys in the center of the handkerchief. Bring up the corners to form a pouch. Clip the corners together with the strong clip.

4. Place the magic wand and confetti into the box. Place the top on the box.

PERFORMANCE:

1. Take out the box and set it on the table. Let the pouch of toys hang behind the table so the audience can't see it. Then smile and say, "I recently found this instant Party in a Box! Who'd like to have a party?"

2. Take the top off. Turn the box sideways to dump out the magic wand and confetti. Be careful not to let the audience see the secret pouch of toys. Look at the confetti and wand in surprise. Say, "Is that it?"

3. Follow these steps to secretly bring the pouch of party toys into the box. First turn the box upside down. Then turn the box toward yourself so the pouch is hanging in the middle of the box (3b). Finally, turn the box right side up so the pouch drops into the box (3c). As you do these motions, pretend to look in the box to search for the "party" inside.

4. Place the top back on the box. Give the audience a disappointed look and say, "This 'Party in a Box' seems like a rip off." Pick up some confetti and toss it in the air with a depressed look.

5. Pick up the wand and look at it. Then pretend to have a sudden idea. Say, "Wait a minute! I wonder what this wand is for?" Wave the wand over the box in a magical way. Pretend that you can hear something happening inside the box.

6. Lift the cover and take a peek inside the box. Give the audience a surprised look and say, "Something magical has happened!" Reach into the box and squeeze the strong clip to release the party toys. Do this with a smooth motion so the audience doesn't guess the secret to the trick.

7. Take out the toys, hand them out to the audience and say, "Now THIS is what I call a party!"

WASHDAY WONDER

Clean up is a breeze with magic soap! The audience will gasp when this special soap instantly takes more than the stains out of a dirty sock.

What You Need:

- a pair of white socks
- a small, empty laundry soap box
- piece of thin cardboard
- a green marker
- scissors

PREPARATION:

1. Use the green marker to draw two large grass "stains" on one sock. Cut two holes in the second sock to match the green spots.

2. Cut the extra piece of cardboard to fit inside the soap box. Place the cardboard in the box to form a secret pocket.

3. Place the sock with the cutout holes inside the secret pocket.

4. Decorate the box to look like special magic soap called "Stain Free."

18

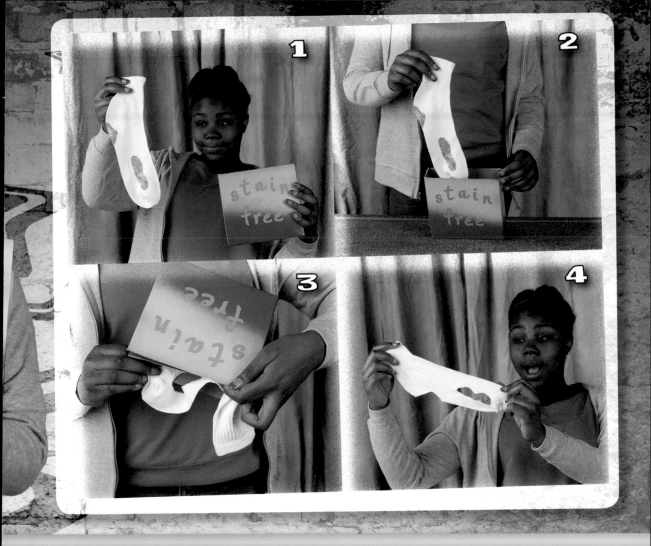

PERFORMANCE:

1. Show the stained sock and the soap box to the audience. Say, "These are some nasty grass stains. I think I'll try some of this new Stain Free soap I found."

2. Place the stained sock into the empty part of the box, and then start shaking it. Tell the audience, "This powerful soap will erase those stains in a flash!"

3. Hold the secret flap against the side of the box to keep the stained sock in place. Dump the secret hidden sock onto the table. Then put away the box.

4. Hold up the sock with holes and say. "Bam! Those grass stains are gone!" Then look closely at the sock. Give a surprised look when you see the large holes in the sock. Tell the crowd, "I guess that magic soap works a little TOO well!"

Ping-Pong Surprise!

Have a bouncy good time making balls appear from nowhere! The audience will love the surprising finish as ping-pong balls suddenly rain down all over you.

What You Need:

o **one large paper bag**
o **scissors**
o **thin cardboard**
o **strong tape**
o **10 to 20 ping-pong balls**
o **magic wand**

PREPARATION:

1. Measure and cut a piece of cardboard to fit inside the bottom of the paper bag.

2. Tape the cardboard inside the bag near the bottom to create a secret flap. Tape the cardboard on one long side so it can flip back and forth inside the bag.

3. Cut a small hole in the back of the bag for your thumb to hold the secret flap.

4. Place the ping-pong balls in the bag under the secret flap. Place a magic wand in the bag on top of the secret flap.

PERFORMANCE:

1. Take out the paper bag and tip it over so the magic wand drops out (1a). Place your thumb or finger through the small hole to keep the secret cardboard flap closed (1b). The audience will believe the bag is empty.

2. With a confused look say, "I thought there was an invisible ball in this bag too." Look around for the invisible ball. Pretend to feel around in front of you to look for the ball. Pretend to find it and hold it up to show the audience.

3. Ask for a volunteer to catch the invisible ball and toss it to him or her. Then ask the person to toss it back into the bag. Pretend to catch the ball with the bag. Repeat this step two more times with other people in the audience.

4. Now ask everyone in the audience to take invisible balls from their pockets and toss them toward you. Pretend that you are trying to catch the balls with the bag. Be sure to keep the secret cardboard flap closed with your thumb. The audience will get a good laugh as you race back and forth trying to catch all of the invisible balls.

5. Finally, wave the magic wand over the bag and say the magic words "Invisibility Reverso!" Lift the bag over your head, turn it over, and look into it. As you do this, let go of the secret flap inside the bag. Act surprised when the balls rain down over you. The crowd will get a kick out of the flood of ping-pong balls falling on your head!

PHOOey SHOey

Don't believe all the ads you see on TV. In this crazy trick, you try to clean a shoe with special cleaner from a TV ad. But instead it becomes an awful mess!

What You Need:

- a large paper bag
- scissors
- a piece of thick cardboard
- an old, beat-up shoe
- a large cardboard box
- an empty soap bottle
- a pillow
- a magic hat
- markers

Polish-All

PREPARATION:

1. Cut a hole in the bottom of the paper bag large enough to fit the shoe through it.

2. Measure and cut the cardboard to fit inside the bottom of the bag. Tape the cardboard in the bag to create a secret flap. Place the old shoe on top of the flap.

3. Decorate the large box to look like a magic table. Cut a flap into the top of the box to match the hole in the bag. Place the pillow and magic hat inside the box.

4. Decorate the soap bottle to look like special cleaner called "Polish–All."

PERFORMANCE:

1. Place the bag on the box over the secret flap. Then look for someone in the audience with shoes similar to the secret shoe. Ask, "May I borrow your shoe? I'd like to try an amazing new product from a TV ad called Polish–All."

2. When someone volunteers a shoe, pretend to place it into the bag. Reach into the bag with one hand and lift up the secret flap and beat up shoe (2a). Use the other hand to drop the volunteer's shoe through the flap in the box and onto the pillow inside (2b). Then let the secret flap inside the bag drop down with the dirty shoe on top of it.

3. Pick up the bottle of "Polish–All" and pretend to squirt some invisible cleaner into the bag.

TIP: Act surprised when you pull out the beat up shoe to add fun for the audience. Sniff it and act like it is disgusting before handing it to the volunteer.

4. Say, "Now we just shake it a little and your shoe should come out sparkling clean!" Shake the bag a bit. Then reach in and pull out the dirty shoe. Hold it up for the volunteer and audience to see.

5. Tell the volunteer, "I guess you can't always trust those TV ads." Ask him or her to wait a moment. Reach into the box and put the volunteer's shoe into the magic hat. Bring out the hat and say, "Thanks for being a good sport. I have a parting gift here for messing up your shoe."

6. Take the shoe out of the hat and hand it to the volunteer. Ask the audience to give the volunteer a round of applause.

Key of Mystery

Where did the key go? When the audience sees a haunted key instantly vanish, they'll start to wonder if ghosts are real!

What You Need:
- a large, old door key
- thin elastic string, about 2 feet (0.6 m) long
- a safety pin
- a jacket with long sleeves

PREPARATION:

1. Tie the key to one end of the elastic string.

2. Attach the other end of the string to the back collar of your jacket with the safety pin.

3. Run the key and string down the inside of your jacket sleeve.

PERFORMANCE:

1. Pretend to reach into your magic case to get the key. You will really be taking the key out from your jacket sleeve. The case will help hide this from the audience.

TIP: Try asking a volunteer to hold the key for you. But as he or she reaches for it, quickly open your hands to show that it has vanished.

2. Hold up the key and show it to the crowd. In a low mysterious voice say, "Legends say this key was found in a haunted castle. They say the ghost of the castle wants it back. Sometimes I feel something tugging on the key as if something is trying to take it away. There—it's happening again!" Pretend that the key is being pulled away from you.

3. Pretend to grab the key with both hands. Cover the key with your second hand (3a). As you do this, secretly allow the key to be pulled up into your jacket sleeve (3b).

4. Open your hands to show the audience that the key has vanished. Tell them, "That ghost must have really needed that key. After all, it was the key to the haunted castle's bathroom!"

T   D ncing   n

Sparky is a friendly hanky that comes to life in a magical way. People will be amazed and amused as they watch his antics on the stage.

TIP: Add more comedy at the end of this trick by placing a third hanky on your back with some tape. When the first hanky flies away, turn around to let the audience see this hanky on your back. People will get a good laugh as they tell you that Sparky is hiding on your back.

What You Need:

- a large cardboard appliance box
- scissors
- a colorful old sheet or tablecloth
- a black hat
- two identical hankerchiefs
- a stick about 2 feet (0.6 meter) long
- tape
- black thread
- a piece of black cloth, 4 inches (10 centimeters) square
- two secret assistants
- a magic wand
- a CD player and some dance music

PREPARATION:

1. Cut a 3-inch (7.6-cm) hole in the top of the large box.

2. Place the sheet over the box and cut a flap to match the hole in the box.

3. Cut another flap into the top of the hat to match the hole in the box.

4. Tape one of the handkerchiefs to one end of the stick.

5. Measure out 20 feet (6 meters) of black thread. Tie one end of the thread to a corner of the second handkerchief.

6. Tape the black cloth inside the hat to form a secret pocket. Leave the top side of the pocket open.

7. One assistant will hide off stage behind the curtains.

8. The second assistant will hide under a table or inside the large box.

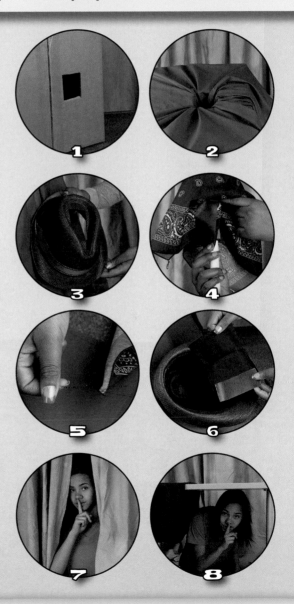

PERFORMANCE:

1. Walk onto the stage holding the hanky attached to the long thread. The thread should run over your elbow and lead off stage to the secret assistant hiding behind the curtain. Tell the audience, "Meet my friend Sparky. He's the world's greatest dancing hanky."

2. Pick up the hat with your other hand and show the audience that it is empty. Place the hat on the box with the secret flap lined up over the secret hole. Say, "Sparky loves this hat. It's his favorite place to hide."

3. Place the hanky in the hat. Tuck it into the secret pocket inside the hat. Leave the corner of the hanky that is tied to the thread at the top of the pocket. Be sure to keep the thread over your elbow.

4. Start the dance music and begin waving the magic wand. The assistant inside the box will poke the hanky on the stick up through the secret hole in the hat. He or she will make the hanky look like it's dancing. Say, "Wow! Those are some crazy dance moves Sparky!"

5. Grab the hanky on the stick and push it back through the hole and down into the box. Say, "That's great Sparky. But it's time to lay down for a nap."

6. After you do this, the assistant hiding off stage will pull on the thread. The first hanky will appear to fly out of the hat, over your arm, and disappear behind the curtain. Tell the audience, "I guess Sparky must be late for his dance lessons!"

READ MORE

Charney, Steve. *The Kids' Guide to Magic Tricks.* Kids' Guides. Mankato, Minn.: Capstone Press, 2013.

Hunter, Nick. *Fun Magic Tricks.* Try This at Home! Chicago: Capstone Raintree, 2013.

Turnbull, Stephanie. *Prop Tricks.* Secrets of Magic. Mankato, Minn.: Smart Apple Media, 2012.

INTERNET SITES

FactHound offers a safe, fun way to find Internet sites related to this book. All of the sites on FactHound have been researched by our staff.

Here's all you do:

Visit *www.facthound.com*

Type in this code: 9781476501369

 Check out projects, games and lots more at
www.capstonekids.com